THIS IS MY STORY...
IS THIS YOUR STORY?

CONFRONTING DEPRESSION AND SUICIDE

Dr. Gilbert G. Campbell, Jr.

Copyright© 2018 by Dr. Gilbert Campell
AcuteByDesign

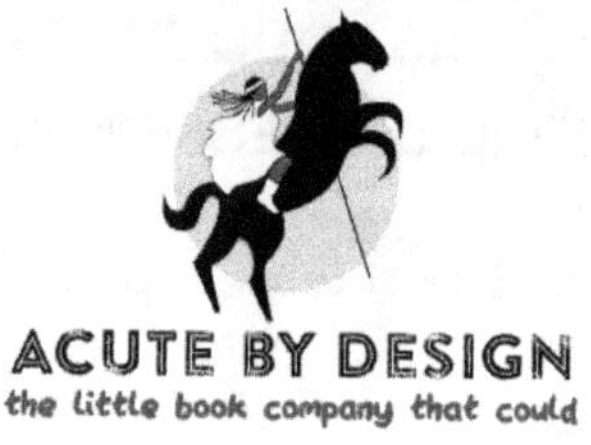

A Michael Marion Sharpe company

ACKNOWLEDGMENTS

This book would not have been written without the support, patience, and love of my family, friends, members of my therapeutic community, and the grace of God. The journey of this work has been wrought with many with many challenges. Yet I have meandered to the finish line because of those aforementioned angels in my life. Thank you for being there for me and being an integral part of this journey.

My late parents, Bertha V. Campbell and Gilbert G. Campbell, Sr., along with my sister, Rosalind C. Taylor, provided and still provide the foundation and tradition out of I which I come. They were and are present at every juncture in my life, whether good or bad. The love and guidance received from them have carried me through the ups and downs of my life.

I have been blessed over the last thirty-eight years of my life to have had three of the best children that a parent could have. Individually and collectively, they have been the center of my joy. Clinical depression never kept me from loving and caring for them. It with joy that I still celebrate their presence in my life. They have become great encouragers in my struggle with my disease and have afforded me their tough love. Gilbert, III; Erica; and Lauren (the shadow) in adulthood have become my best friends and the reason for being.

There have been many family members and friends who have been there for me throughout the years. My love for you remains constant, and your friendship validates that it does take a "village." I can only hope that I can and will remain the loyal, trusted friend that you have been to me.

Veranda Dickens, thanks for your continuous insight, guidance, and presence in my life. You have understood my disease and at the same time been a strong personality in my life. Mere words cannot express what you have meant to me. I pray that our friendship and relationship will continue to grow.

To the AcuteByDesign family, Michael Marion Sharpe, Executive Publisher; Cynthia MacGregor, Editorial Operations Executive; and the entire staff of a great publishing company, thank you so much for working with me in publishing my first work. I am grateful for your faith and trust in me in my attempt to "save one life" by telling "My Story."

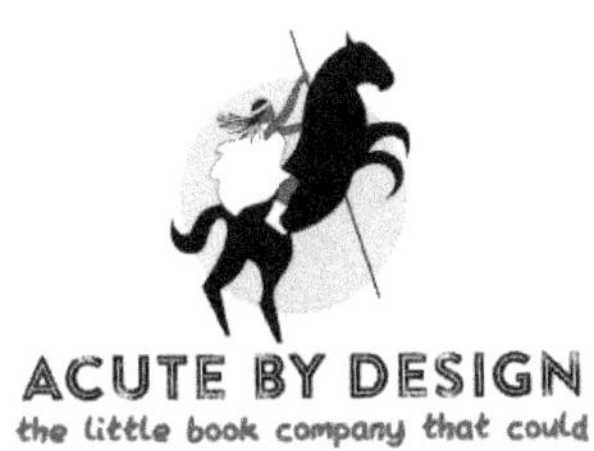

ACUTE BY DESIGN
the little book company that could

A Michael Marion Sharpe company

To produce and publish high quality diverse, multicultural, and socially relevant books for children and young readers; their teachers, and parents

To provide opportunities for teachers and under-represented writers and illustrators to publish their dream book, and

To provide small grants to teachers and parent associations to help provide resources for underserved students and classrooms.

Thank you for helping to make that dream come true for so many!

Michael Marion Sharpe
Publisher

www.acutebydesign.com

PREFACE

"Child, ain't nothing wrong with that boy! He just has the vapors." These were the words of a beloved mother describing the many moods of her only son. The writer heard those words all too often as he lived with clinical depression without being aware until he reached his forty-seventh year of existence. It makes one wonder how could a person live forty-seven years of his life without an awareness that he was living with depression. Sir Winston Churchill called depression "the black dog." Other writers have referred to depression as "the beast."

I can understand and empathize with those references to depression. For me, depression has been a lifelong journey of dealing with the ups and downs of this tumultuous disease. In this book, I am going to chronicle the story of the son of a preacher and educator who has struggled with this disease throughout his earthly sojourn.

This painful work is, first of all, an attempt to save just one life from suicide, and second, to assist all of my brothers and sisters who live with this disease daily, help those who are not aware that they suffer from depression, and assist others in understanding the pain of their loved one who lives with depression.

I have reached a point in my life where the scales and shackles have been lifted. I am ready and poised to risk a great deal in sharing this life story of a college-trained and seminary-prepared Baptist preacher, one who has pastored successfully for many years.

The old folk used to say, "Talk about me as much as you please. The more you talk about me, I am going to bend my knees." I am writing this book with the blessings of my three children, my sister, family members, friends, colleagues, congregants, psychiatrist, therapists, social workers, physicians, and fellow sufferers.

In the words of the great gospel singer Mahalia Jackson, and the writer of this great inspirational song, composer Alma Bazel Androzza:

"If I can help somebody as I pass along,
If I can cheer somebody with a word or song,
If I can show somebody that he's travelling wrong,
Then my living will not be in vain."

Contents

CHAPTER ONE
THIS IS MY STORY

"Walking this lonesome valley."

After forty-seven years, I was diagnosed with clinical depression by a team of psychiatrists in a Washington, DC hospital. This pronouncement sounded like the end of the world to me. My first response was, "Should I come out of work on disability?"

Their response was, "Hell, no! Look at the many marvelous things you have done in your life without the knowledge that you were living with depression." The next hour or so, I listened as they shared with me what clinical depression was and how it presented itself in my life. They stated that clinical depression was oft-times hereditary and inquired if any of my family members had been diagnosed with this disease. Initially, I could not readily think of anyone in my family of origin, but after some time alone, I realized there was a history of suicide, alcoholism, and family members who exhibited other signs of depression.

I called both of my parents and asked them about depression in their respective families, and both them denied knowing of any family member who had lived with depression. This brought about feelings of anger and resentment at both of them as I recalled for them a sibling who blew his brains out with an elephant rifle, siblings who were alcoholics, and siblings who would retreat with feelings of despondency. It became clear to me that I had to educate my generation of the family regarding this inherited disease. As a successful pastor, who had received a Bachelor's Degree in social work, a Master of Divinity Degree from one of the finest theological schools in the Boston area, and a Doctor of Ministry Degree, and studied at some of this world's great universities, that I had to share my story with others. This was done through sermons, workshops, and in individual and family counseling sessions. My story was being told with my academic training and ability to effectively communicate the story. Yet, I never really shared the entire story, a story that needs to be told.

Looking back, I recall that the "vapors," or my depression, began during my teen years. I would retreat to my bedroom and just stay in bed. There was no control over the long periods of retreating from family and no factors contributing to this isolation. I did not grow up in a broken home, had supportive parents and an older sister who was a positive role model for me. As I grew up African-American in Virginia during the days of segregation, my parents, both educated and intelligent, loving and supportive, provided a wholesome environment for my sister and me.

Living in a middle-class environment, all of our needs were met, and there was always a family vacation, of course, in the northern cities and Canada. Those trips would always culminate with a stop in New York City. We stayed in the most luxurious hotels and dined at the best restaurants. There was Broadway, shopping sprees, and the sights and sounds of that great city, but the highlight for me was my father and me walking out of the hotel, summoning a cab, and my hearing him say, "Yankee Stadium."

During my teen years, there were no external causative red flags for depression. Yet, it would constantly raise its ugly head on a regular basis. I was very popular in high school, had good friends, was a star on the basketball team, a very good student, and popular with the girls, but I still had many moments of severe isolation (depression). My struggle with depression continued on throughout my college and graduate studies, when I was always finding myself alone and aloof. There was not one person in my life aware of my depression. I have realized since my diagnosis that mental illness was taboo during those days and no one would talk about it anywhere.

The first recognizable occurrence I can recall was after I accepted the invitation to become the senior pastor of one of the largest churches in Winston-Salem, NC, at the age of twenty-six.

I thought I could handle such a huge assignment because at the age of twenty-three, I had already successfully pastored a small, inner city church in the Roxbury section of Boston, MA. Armed with that experience, a Master of Divinity with honors in hand, the Outstanding Preaching and Promise in Parish Ministry Award conferred upon graduation, as a third-generation pastor, I was ready to conquer the world.

Upon my arrival in Winston-Salem, I was received with great excitement, and the expectations were challenging. The church experienced tremendous growth—spiritually, financially, and numerically. For twenty-six years, academically and professionally, I was on the fast track. The one constant factor in my life was my mood swings, which I began to think were normal and that I was just a loner. All of that changed within two years, and all hell broke out in my life!

My first year in Winston-Salem was filled with many achievements, and the marriage between pastor/people blossomed tremendously. I was going through the ebb and flow of my work, being innovative, building up the great work of a pastor emeritus who had served for thirty years in the church, which had been founded in 1879. I became only their fourth pastor. In their historical narrative, this is said of my time there: "With the arrival in 1979 of the Reverend Gilbert G. Campbell, Jr., a native of Richmond, Virginia, as its fourth pastor, Mount Zion experienced more growth, enhanced love of church, and program expansion. Under his management and objective leadership style, Reverend Campbell institutionalized an annual church budget and encouraged Mount Zion to make more financial investments with its capital holdings. The Inspirational Choir, Audio-Video ministry, Handbell choirs, new members' class, Sacred Music Institute, and the Athletic Association were enhanced, which prompted Mount Zion's refrain: We Are One in the Spirit."

How ironic! Nothing is mentioned of the experience and situation that caused my first major encounter with depression. After being there over a year, I experienced what F. Scott Fitzgerald has called, "In a real dark night of the soul it is always three o'clock in the morning, day after day." The genesis of this turmoil began when the administrative assistant of the church called me one evening while I was attending a conference in Houston, TX, cursing and complaining, in reference to a proposal I was working on to improve the management of the church, change the internal and external financial controls of the church, and implement a plan to ascertain more congregation participation in all facets of congregational life.

I knew from the tenor and tone of the conversation that she had to be directly confronted on that kind of disrespect. In our personal meeting, she displayed no remorse over our previous conversation and refused to discuss the proposed policy and managerial changes that a congregational-approved committee and I had been working on to present back to the church. Her confrontational attitude toward me presented me with no other alternative but to fire her. A meeting was called with leaders of the church, and after a lengthy meeting with them, they informed me that she had been with the church for twenty-seven years and that I needed to find a way to work with her.

I went to the pastor emeritus for consultation, and he shared with me that he was "observing" and wanted to see how I would deal with that situation. I could not understand why a seasoned, highly successful pastor, a living legacy, and one with a reputation of integrity would not offer his services to her or me. I left his house feeling bitter toward him. From that moment, he began to interfere with my ministry at that church. The administrative assistant and her supporters launched a smear campaign.

At twenty-seven years of age, I was not prepared for that kind of conflict. I had grown up in a conflict-free home, excelled academically, prepared myself for ministry, and had gotten along well with people. I had experienced mood swings, but nothing like I felt at that time. I had not offended anyone nor done any of those things the rumor and gossip mills accused me of doing. After months of inner turmoil, pain, and as I recall now (though I didn't recognize it while I was experiencing it then), a very severe depressive period in my life. This depression caused great feelings of hopelessness and despair. I saw no way out! The only resolution I felt was for me to resign and leave and escape the situation. This I did. I got the hell out of there!

The congregation would not accept my resignation. Eighty percent of the members present voted not to accept it. But by then, it was too late for me to stay. I did not see the congregational support. My despair and depression were too great. I had to leave!

After leaving that church and prior to accepting a senior pastor position in Philadelphia, PA, I felt like a failure, desired to quit the ministry, and in my deep depression, like others in the Bible, I told God that I would not speak for Him again. At my lowest point, I had suicidal ideations for the first time. When I resigned upon recommendation from my father, I had asked the congregation to do an external audit because of the need to do one in the change of administration. I was not expecting any negative things to come out of this examination. The church had experienced tremendous financial growth and had invested well under my leadership.

There I was, contemplating getting out of the ministry and committing suicide, when I received a call from a leader in church informing me that the administrative assistant was found to have embezzled thousands of dollars over a three-year period. She died shortly after that, and I began to pull out of that dark period in my life. I was ready to move on, knowing why this person, whom I had never offended, had sought to ruin my name, my character, and my career. To this day, it is my feeling that the pastor emeritus was involved in this cover-up, for she had worked for him for over twenty years.

I received phone calls from the church leadership inquiring if I desired to return to the church. Thinking about returning brought about more feelings of depression. I moved on! Yes, moving on, I thought, was a good thing, but I discovered that in the ebb and flow of my work, whenever faced with conflict and confrontation, I would retreat to my cocoon and remain in the bed or isolate myself from family and people. The monster of depression would be back again.

Over the next thirty-plus years, I have had many highs and lows, ups and downs, depression-free years and years when I often found myself depressed on a regular basis. Therapy and anti-depressants proved to be an effective course of treatment. In retrospect, I have always faithfully taken my meds but seldom received therapeutic intervention. Conflict and confrontation produced many years of pain, hopelessness, despair, broken relationships, and numerous suicide attempts. It is difficult for me to believe that I have had: twelve hours of vascular surgery (aortobifemoral bypass) on my legs, two heart attacks, fifteen stent placements, three hospitalizations following suicide attempts, divorces, permanent disability at the age of fifty-four, Type-2 diabetes, and many more significant life events. I will in subsequent chapters share many of my depressive episodes throughout my life and, more importantly, attempt to assist you on your journey.

This is my story, but my story may be your story.

CHAPTER TWO
THIS IS YOUR STORY

Can I get a witness? Have you had any of these symptoms of depression? Symptoms such as: prolonged sadness, sleeplessness or periods of prolonged sleeping, unexplained crying spells, irritability, mood swings, extended lethargy, feelings of worthlessness, worry, anxiety, loss of energy, drug or alcohol abuse, overeating (bulimia) or under-eating (anorexia), inability to concentrate, unexplained aches and pains, indifference, pessimism, lost of interest in in pleasurable things, aloofness, and thoughts of death and suicide. If so, you may be a member of my "family," a family of over 300 million co-sufferers of depression worldwide, and over fifteen million nationwide. Welcome to the family!

This is a family that includes celebrities, dignitaries, and luminaries such as former presidents: John Adams, Thomas Jefferson, James Madison, John Quincy Adams, Franklin Pierce, Abraham Lincoln, and Calvin Coolidge. Also, in the family are: Beyonce, T.I, Kendra Lamar, Alicia Keys, Kanye West, Janet Jackson, Ashley Judd, Owen Wilson, Hallie Berry, Dwayne "The Rock" Johnson, Lady Gaga, Catherine Zeta-Jones, Wayne Brady, Kerry Washington, Sheryl Crow, Princess Diana, Sir Winston Churchill, Mark Twain, and many others.

In this family, you will find people from all walks, stations, professions, ethnicities, economic statuses, age groups, and religious backgrounds. One cannot physically or visually determine if a person is depressed. It is easy for one to mask their depression by smiling while they are hurting, or appearing fine one day and committing suicide the next. I remember constantly going through the ebb and flow of life, functioning extremely well while at the same time concealing my thoughts and pains, and feeling one or more of the symptoms of depression. There are many forms of depression. You can be diagnosed with:
- Major Depressive Disorder
- Dysthymia (clinical or chronic)

- Situational Depression
- Atypical (bipolar) Depression
- Seasonal Affective Disorder
- Catatonic Depression
- Psychotic Depression
- Peripartum (Postpartum) Depression
- Premenstrual Dysphoric Disorder
- Melancholic Depression
- Adjustment Disorder

Major Depressive Disorder can be best described as having five or more of the symptoms on most days for two weeks or longer. The symptoms must involve a depressed mood or loss of activities. Dysthymia is less severe than major depression and has fewer symptoms than major depression, usually lasting two or more years or longer. Situational Depression is a short-term form of depression that can occur following traumatic changes in your life, including divorce, loss of a job, or the death of a relative or dear friend. Atypical depression (bipolar) affects how you feel, think, and behave, and can lead to emotional and physical problems. This makes it difficult to perform normal day-to-day activities, and often brings to the surface suicidal ideations and even actual suicide or at least an attempt. Psychotic Depression is known as depressive disorder. Some people who experience this have hallucinations, false beliefs, and a loss of contact with reality. Seasonal Affective Disorder emerges during particular seasons of the year and recurs around the same time each year, sapping one of energy and often making you feel moody. Peripartum (Postpartum) Depression often occurs in women following childbirth. Women will feel sad, blue, and depressed as a result of giving birth to a child. Premenstrual Dysphoric Disorder is related to premenstrual symptoms (PMS) in women, and may cause mood swings, breast tenderness, headache, irritability, hot flashes, food cravings, fatigue, panic attacks, joint pain, or frequent crying. Melancholic Depression is a form of depression that is often related to the inability to find pleasure in positive things, mood swings, severe weight loss, psychomotor agitation or retardation, early morning awakening, and guilt that is excessive, with the worst mood occurring in the morning. The final form of depression for our sharing is Adjustment Disorder, a short-term condition that occurs when a person has great difficulty coping with, or adjusting to, a particular source of stress, such as a major life change, loss, or event. Please keep in mind that any of the aforementioned types of depression can be very dangerous to one's life if untreated. Remember, you are not alone in your struggles with depression.

Depression knows no face, ethnicity, religious preference, gender, or class distinction. It can affect anyone at any age, including children, adolescents, adults, and the elderly. An estimated one in ten Americans suffer annually from the disease. A major cause for depression can also be cancer, strokes, heart attacks, HIV, Parkinson's disease, eating disorders, substance abuse, and diabetes. Caregivers who care for their elder relatives often find themselves with significant depressive symptoms. Some researchers believe that women experience depression at twice the rate of men. Major depressive disorders are one of the leading top three causes of disability in the workplace issues, following only family crisis and stress. This results in lost workdays and decreased productivity due to the symptoms that sap energy, affect work habits, and cause problems with concentration, memory, and decision-making.

I am writing this book not just to be informative about the disease but to encourage you who are or may be suffering from some form of depression to get the necessary assistance to aid you in living a productive and healthy life in spite of the disease. There's no one proven method that helps people recover from depression; it's different for everyone. You can get a range of effective treatments, and health professionals who can help you on the road to recovery. If this is your story, the most important thing is finding the right treatment and the right health professional for your needs. Again, welcome to the family!

CHAPTER THREE
THIS IS OUR STORY

Our story is suffering through many types and degrees of depression. Our story is navigating through the maze that cripples us mentally, physically, and socially. Our story is trying to figure out when this dark cloud hovering over us will dissipate. Our story centers on how the beast of depression weighs us down and paralyzes us from day to day. Our story manifests itself in many painful ways. Our story is the absence in our lives of joy and peace of mind. Our story is a matter of life and death.

Do you desire to move on to a good place and space, where life takes on a new meaning? If so, confess and acknowledge that you may have some form of depression. Please refrain from self-analyzing and self-diagnosing your condition. The best manner to begin dealing with your situation is to seek professional assistance from a psychiatrist, psychologist, social worker, physician, or therapist. In seeking professional help, you may discover that this is not your story. Everybody feels depressed at some juncture in life, but that does not mean a diagnosis of depression fits you. Procrastination will not provide you with the answers you are seeking and surely will not get you out of the pit of depression.

My lifelong battle with depression has been evolving from one degree to another. For years, from my teen years and early adulthood, I meandered through life with no idea of what was going on with me. Depression will raise up its ugly head in different ways and at different times. In retrospect, it can come during and after a great crisis, following great accomplishments, and often with no significant causative factors. In recent years, I am now totally aware when a depressive bout appears, and it arises when I am stressed or in a crisis. Please understand that without diagnosis, treatment, and therapy, the aforementioned types of depression can literally make your life miserable from day to day until you reach a breaking point. I cannot stress enough the importance of reaching out to professionals who can guide you through your depression. You may experience situational depression from any of the following experiences:

- Death of a significant other or loved one
- Divorce or break-up with a significant other
- Loss of job or stress on the job
- Relational dysfunctions at home, with friends, work, school, etc.
- Being a primary caregiver
- Illness, or illness of a loved one
- Financial woes
- Physical or sexual assault, combat, or natural disaster
- Hormonal abnormalities

You will discover that therapeutic intervention from a friend, family member, physician, psychiatrist, therapist, clergyperson, etc., can often provide a temporary or lasting relief from situational depression. Prayer and other modalities are always healthy approaches, but I have found that reaching out to professionals provides a more systemic manner of working on your situation. This is your story!

If you are not sure what type of depression you are experiencing, please reach out to the therapeutic community to determine whether or not you are dealing with a chemical form of depression, in which case you need to be more aggressive in reaching out for help. Failing to do so can lead to your life spiraling out of control. Chemical depression will never disappear, but it can be managed on a day-to-day basis with appropriate assistance from those who can provide you will the professional help that you so badly need. This will prevent you from destroying yourself emotionally, financially, relationally, and physically.

Reach out before the pain becomes so great that feelings of despair and hopelessness overwhelm you. Let me caution you from a personal perspective: There is more pain and hopelessness in thinking that you have the resolution to your dysfunction. My life would get out of control, would affect negatively those among my social contacts, and would often get me thinking of suicide or actually attempting suicide. This has been my story and could be your story, if it is not already your story.

Our story is a painful story but not a defining story. We can live with, deal with, and work through depression. If you are reading this book and feel that you need to reach out, please do so. Don't allow the stigma of depression and a mental health disease cause you to refrain from reaching to those who can assist you on your journey. This is our story, and we are in this together. I am pleading with you to walk this painful and lonesome valley with me.

I am also urging you to do what is necessary to remove this veil of darkness that can be and or is ruining your story. My story is in print, and I can no longer hide the fact that I have lived with depression all my life. I am writing to you so that you can take that step forward and acknowledge and affirm a possible diagnosis of depression that can lift you out of the quicksand, allow you to live a productive life, and possibly save your life. Choose to live a productive life. Choose to fight and not succumb to the possibility that depression can destroy. Choose to make your story our story.

People from all walks of life, the professional, the blue collar, the housewife, or the unemployed and the unemployable, the addict, the teacher, the clergyperson, the physician, the psychiatrist, the psychologist, the police officer, the sanitation worker, the alcoholic, the politician, the athlete, the entertainer... the list goes on and on. You are not different from any human who suffers with depression, treated or untreated.

I have found in my life that depression can be debilitating, destructive, disruptive, and disheartening. I fight daily to not allow depression to take over my life. It is hard but not impossible. I have to engage in this battle daily to avoid staying in bed, not being productive, and living an anti-social existence. It is very comfortable to allow depression to take control over my life. You and I have too much to offer to live handicapped by a very treatable disease. It's treatable, but you have to assertively confront this beast daily. There are times I want to stay in bed, not deal with life, and avoid relationships that are beneficial. This is why I write so fervently: You are important to me, and an integral part of my life.

I may not know your name but I know your story, because your story and my story are our story. I can empathize with you, and I have walked the road that you are walking. Help and hope can be on the way, only if you decide that you have had enough. The journey will not be easy, but it will be very rewarding. I am glad that my suicide attempts were all failures, and from those painful moments I have learned that I am a survivor who has a great deal to offer. People may not understand your journey, but there are some of us who are cognizant of your struggles and battles. You can live a good and joyous life even with depression. Depression is not a demon or some self-imposed dungeon that one chooses to live in. Remember, depression is a treatable disease that can be managed, and it is not a death sentence.

Many of us in this struggle find it very difficult to reach out for the help we so badly need. Reach out to someone you can trust and confide in: a significant other, a family member, a friend, a co-worker, a physician, a clergy member, or anyone who can guide you through this maze. They will gladly lead you to a professional. As noted previously, you cannot heal yourself. People who love you do not want you to linger in a sea of hopelessness and despair.

I called a denominational official, who confidently led me to a mental health hospital 200 miles away from my home and the church that I was pastoring. It was the best place for me at that horrific time in my life. I was in a confined environment, which allowed me the opportunity to focus on my situation. It was there I was diagnosed with clinical depression. I was educated about the disease by a psychiatrist and therapist. There I received individual and group therapy and informational books and pamphlets. Daily I found myself wanting more information and aggressively invested in the treatment that I was receiving.

My stay there was a painful but rewarding experience. They worked with me prior to my discharge in finding a psychiatrist and a support system to assist in managing the disease. Seventeen years later, I have in place a psychiatrist and therapist to assist me in my continuous struggle with the disease. The first and last thing I do daily is take my anti-depressant medications.

Our story is never-ending, and we will never defeat the disease unless we are constantly and consistently engaging in our treatment. We often feel that we are feeling and functioning better, that we do not need to take our medications, and hence, we stop seeing our therapist and psychiatrist. Living with depression is an ongoing battle and lengthy struggle. Feeling that you do not need to continue to do the things that were beneficial to your well-being and recovery is very dangerous.

This is our story, and we must be diligent on our journey so that we can live rich and productive lives.

CHAPTER FOUR
THIS IS OUR HOUSE

"I was wounded in the house of my friends" ~ Zechariah 13:6

Residing in our house are our parents or guardians, significant others, children, and friends. These are people who love us and yet, at the same time, can be the causative factors in our ongoing struggle with depression. We are the ones who are affected by depression, and we often inflict our pain on others. Consciously or subconsciously, we are the ones causing conflict or dysfunction in our family of origin and with those in our current families, extended families, and friends.

The disease may be ours to claim, but oft-times we fail to inform those who care and love us of our situation. It is extremely important that we make them aware of our struggle. They can possibly provide guidance to the people who can assist us. You do not have to fight this battle alone, and remember, your life is important to them as well as to yourself. Self-awareness and reaching out to others are great places to start in moving forward to your well-being and treatment of your depression. I have discovered in my personal bouts of depression that the sooner I become cognizant of what I am feeling and share it with others, the sooner I can get started with my treatment, avoiding a prolonged and painful bout.

Those in your household who have been with you on this journey often recognize when you are relapsing and spiraling downward into a dysfunctional season of depression. I thank God for my three loving and caring children, who have educated themselves on my disease and will confront me when they feel that my depression is resurfacing. They can see through my attempts to mask my feelings and will work together in encouraging me to get some help. I am here solely because of them and their acceptance of the fact that their father has clinical depression.

Whatever type of depression you have, you will need a caring, supportive, patient, and loving community of family, friends, co-workers, or others who have been diagnosed with the disease.

One of the major pitfalls we deal with is denial, and another is embarrassment. I deny to myself that I am going down this road of depression again. The pain is so great, and there is no quick fix or magical pill to keep you from relapsing. I have found that being faithful to my medicines and maintaining regular visits to the therapist keep the monster away. I am learning that when in crisis, I need to be more aggressive in seeing my psychiatrist and therapist. This lessens the blow and gives me the professional support I need. Depression will make you an isolationist, but I caution you to fight the urge to closet yourself away from others. On the other hand, avoid the negative people, enablers, and people who are not encouragers.

Again, depression is treatable, and one should tend to it. It is a common problem, and you should not be shamed about seeking help. Depression, like any medical malady, changes one's lifestyle and should be managed in a healthful manner. We can live with this disorder as long as we are mindful of the need for continued care and management. You are not alone, and your loved ones need to go along with you on this journey.

On the other hand, there are significant others, family, friends, and co-workers who are uninformed, mean-spirited, cruel, and not compassionate or caring in relating to us and the disease. I have found that in personal relationships, your significant other often struggles with your disease because first impressions are lasting. They meet and get to know you when you are feeling and doing well. They are unaware of the darks days and significant mood swings depression brings upon us. When depressed, we shy away from social interaction and avoid crowds and people in general.

When I am well, they see the part of me that is handling the disease. If I am interested in getting to know someone better, I always share my struggles with depression, initially, but most of the time, they fail to see you in a depressed mood and forget that you are a person living with some form of depression. They enjoy the relationship until you are in a serious storm associated with the disease. It does not matter how well informed one is regarding the disease; for most people, first impressions are lasting.

A covenant needs to be made between your significant others and you. This covenant involves the self-realization of the onset of a depressive mood and of their realization of a change in your mood or your withdrawal. The honesty of the covenant is so important in that the wheels toward treatment start early, and the avoidance of a major depression can occur. For me, recognizing that I am a little down, and my assertiveness in talking to a significant other can lead to the early cessation of my inward withdrawal from others, and at the same time improve my overall well-being.

When challenged by a significant other regarding their observance of a mood swing in me, it is important that I hear them and begin to discuss with them where I am personally and possibly my need to reach out to my professional helping community. Professionally, I became adept at masking my depression but would withdraw from my family and friends on a personal basis. By nature, I am a caring and loving person in my work and in my relationships, but the ones who were part of my family suffered the most. The importance of a covenant between significant others keeps our relationship on an even keel. The keel on a ship keeps it calm and stable, and the keel in your life keeps you calm and stable. Your covenant with others becomes the key for dealing with your depression inwardly and outwardly. There are times in our lives that our spouses and significant others reject our depression. Painfully, this occurs when we fail to get the assistance we need, and remain in a long period of depression. On the other hand, they may have some significant issues in their own lives and may not have the wherewithal to reach out to you. They become non-caring, mean-spirited, and will withdraw from you on a continuous basis. This causes a great deal of pain in the relationship and can lead to your sinking into a deeper state of depression.

You should always remember that you should make your well-being the primary focus in dealing with your depression and avoid blaming others as the causative factor. When the pain is afflicted by a significant other, it is more lasting, and you have to be more assertive in reaching out to your psychiatrist or therapist. When hurt by a significant other, I would often withdraw and sink into a deeper bout of depression.

In your relationships with significant others, you may find that some will intentionally seek to keep you in a state of depression to take advantage of you. These are mean-spirited people; it will take your helping community to get you to understand that they are carrying so much baggage of their own that will not know how to be in a caring relationship with another and, to say the least, one who is suffering with depression. Breaking free from that relationship can be an enabling factor in getting you out of that state of depression and moving on with your life. You should never allow anyone to keep you in a constant state of depression. On the other hand, when you are struggling with situational depression, remember family and friends mean well but are not the best people in helping you out of this kind of depression. As a pastor, I have heard many people attempt to encourage others with statements like "Be strong," or "It's going to get better." For you in that period of your life, those words don't mean one earthly thing because the situation is overwhelming you.

A person who has had a meaningful and impactful relationship on your life has died, you are going through a painful divorce or a stressful period in a relationship, you have lost your job and the stress of job-hunting is so burdensome, you have relocated to a new area and left your network of friends, or some other traumatic event in your life has occurred, and those who know you say, "Be strong," or "It's going to get better," but these are people you should avoid. It can be a very painful and stressful period in your life if you don't get the professional help you need to assist you in confronting the situation or circumstance that has you wallowing in this kind of state of depression. When you are able to overcome situational depression, it helps you to better prepare for that crisis that is a part of life.

We have all been "wounded in the house of our friends."

31

CHAPTER 5
THIS IS OUR PAIN

In life, nobody likes to experience any kind of physical pain. Our bodily pain can come in the form of a headache, backache, toothache, bone discomfort, or any of a number of other maladies that render us uncomfortable and in need of some form of relief. The relief may come in some form of medications, prescribed or over the counter. All we want is for the pain to go away. We will go to any extreme to alleviate the kind of physical pain that can be debilitating. We just desire to feel and function better in our daily activities. When the medication does not help us in dealing with the pain, we will often seek physical therapy or some other form of pain management simply because we hate pain.

The type or form of depression we may be suffering from can be as debilitating as physical pain. Depression hurts like hell! I would encourage you to refer back to Chapter 2 and get a firm grasp of how the disease works. The psychosocial pain is with you twenty-four hours a day. The pain is so great that you may stay in bed all day, avoid relationships all day, find it difficult to stay focused at work or school...and in general, the pain just makes your life miserable. For me, the pain of depression is far greater than any physical pain I have experienced.

The good news is that you do not have to remain in pain. It is important that you reach out and not let the pain linger. The longer the pain persists, the more difficult it will be to work your way out of it. Self-medicating the pain through drugs, alcohol, overeating, staying in bed, or social withdrawal is not the answer, and closeting yourself will drive you into a deeper state of depression. The only way out of it is to personally own up to it and reach out to your significant others, psychiatrist, and therapist. We believe that the pain will go away without doing something positive about it. I have never worked myself out of it by self-treating.

In addition, physical symptoms are common in depression, and in fact, aches and pain are often the presenting symptoms of depression. The symptoms include joint pain, limb pain, back pain, gastrointestinal issues, tiredness, sleep disturbances, psychomotor activity changes, and appetite changes. There is a link between depression and muscle tension that has been established by many professionals. The physical changes caused by depression can trigger or worsen depression. On the other hand, depression can cause pain and pain can cause depression.

Some research shows that pain and depression share common pathways in the limbic region in the brain. In fact, the same chemical messengers control pain and mood. Many people suffering from depression never get help because they don't realize that pain may be a symptom of depression. Remember, you feel pain because you're depressed, and you're depressed because you're in pain.

Depression is a mental pain that causes great mental torment. For one who has not experienced the torment of depression, it is difficult to put the pain in words. It cannot be described as a stabbing, shooting, or burning pain; neither can the sensations be localized to any one part of the body. It is a crucifying pain that slowly permeates every fiber of one's being. Falling prey to a depressive illness is not like being hit by a car; it is more akin to being eating alive by an army of flesh-eating bacteria. I have experienced many physical maladies, but none greater than the inner pain associated with my depression.

The pain of depression can last decades in unrelenting emotional inner pain despite many forms of intervention. Most depression numbs emotion, especially grief, despair, fear, anger, and shame. We become accustomed to stashing away feelings that have no outlet for expression. The suppression of these pain emotions become entrenched, a habit, and a way of living. Instead of looking for a quick fix for the inner pain you experience, work hard on getting to the root of the problem. Journeying through this vicious type of pain is not a sprint but a long, tedious marathon race. It is one that can be successfully completed with a determination to invest yourself totally into your mental well-being by having consciousness of your need for therapy, medications, and surrounding yourself with positive people.

The pain you are experiencing from your particular type of depression is real. You have to be very aggressive in confronting your pain to avoid a prolonged bout or recurrence of the dark, dismal pit of depression. It does not matter how great the pain—it must be dealt with in an aggressive manner. When you avoid and deny the pain that you are experiencing, it will only make your recovery more difficult and the depression even more severe. Your way out is only a phone call away, and delaying that call is a life-or-death matter. Reaching out for help is the first step in alleviating the pain.

The second step is to be totally honest about your state of mind. I have found that when I reach out to my psychiatrist or therapist and open up in honesty, it makes it easier for those in the helping profession to assess where you are and immediately prescribe the right kind of treatment for you. I often use the analogy of "pulling teeth" as in a dentist struggling to remove an unhealthy tooth. Being honest is the best method in dealing with the disease of depression.

Please keep in mind that you are dealing with a disease that is manageable, and you can find relief from your pain. Reaching out and being honest is not a sign of weakness but of strength. I can attest that these first two steps in dealing with your depression and confronting this disease are a great starting point in rebounding and regaining your well-being, and this leads to the final step.

I cannot stress the importance of maintaining the realistic goals that you and those in your helping community have set for your ongoing treatment plan. Your depression will be with you for a while if it is situational, and all other forms of depression are lasting. One finds hope in knowing that you can go on and live a successful lifestyle. This can be accomplished only by understanding the steps that you have boldly taken to confront your depression. Your goals should include: keeping appointments with your psychiatrist and therapist, taking your medicines on a constant basis, avoiding stressful situations and circumstances, and maintaining a healthy lifestyle in terms of your diet, exercise, and work habits. I know that much of what I am saying sounds redundant, but this is my story and your story of depression.

CHAPTER 6
THIS IS NOT THE WAY OUT!—SUICIDE

Is suicide the easiest way to overcome your form or type of depression? Is suicide the best option for you in this season of hopelessness, despair, and despondency? Can you navigate your way through the deep, dark, and dirty waters that have you to the point of taking your own life? Have you reached the point of no return in your daily struggle to live a wholesome and productive life? Are you currently contemplating and deliberating in your own mind your desire to take your own life? Has the prospect of suicide been a dark cloud over your life for a while? Please allow me the opportunity to delve into these questions throughout this chapter from a personal perspective and educate you on this painful subject. Come walk with me through this precarious subject that has impacted my life and may have done the same to yours in some way. Whether you have had suicidal ideations, attempted suicide, or had a significant other, family member, friend, neighbor, or co-worker actually attempt or succeed and die from suicide, come struggle with me through this chapter.

Suicide has been very prevalent in my life. A maternal uncle actually killed himself by placing an elephant rifle to his head in the sixties; friends have taken their lives along with fellow clergy and members of my churches; and in my struggle with clinical depression I have often had suicidal ideations and suicidal attempts. Suicide in some manner has impacted all of our lives. Suicide can be defined as the act of intentionally taking one's life.

Suicide Statistics
- Suicide is the tenth leading cause of death in the United States for all ages.
- Every day, approximately 105 Americans die by suicide.
- There is one death by suicide in the United States every 12 minutes.
- Depression affects 20-25 percent of Americans ages

eighteen and over.
- Suicide takes the lives of 38,000 Americans every year.
- The highest suicide rates in the United States are among Whites, American Indians, and Alaska Natives.
- Suicide is the second leading cause of death in the world for those ages fifteen through twenty-four.
- There is one death by suicide in the world every forty seconds.
- An estimated quarter of a million people each year become suicide survivors in the United States.
- There is one suicide for every estimated twenty-five suicide attempts in the United States.
- There is one suicide for every estimated four suicide attempts in the elderly.
- Suicide by males is four times higher than by females. Male deaths represent 79 percent of all United States suicides.
- Females attempt suicide three times as often as males.
- One in 100,000 children ages ten to fourteen die by suicide each year.
- Seven in 100,000 youths ages fifteen to nineteen die by suicide each year.
- Twelve and seven-tenths in 100,000 young adults ages twenty through twenty-four die by suicide each year.
- Suicide is the third leading cause of death for fifteen- to twenty-four-year-old Americans.
- Suicide is the fourth leading cause of death for adults ages eighteen to sixty-five.
- The highest increase in suicide is in males fifty and over, at a rate of thirty per 100,000 Americans.
- Suicide rates for females are highest among those aged forty-five through fifty-four.
- Suicide rates for males is highest for males seventy-five and over.
- Suicide rates among the elderly are highest for those who are divorced or widowed.
- Lesbian, gay, and bisexual kids are three times more likely

than straight kids to attempt suicide at some point in their lives.
• African American, Latino, Native American, and Asian people who are lesbian, gay, or bisexual attempt suicide at especially high rates.
• Forty-one percent of trans adults said they had attempted suicide, and sixty-one percent of trans people who were victims of physical assault have attempted suicide.
• There were more than twice as many suicides (44,193) in the United States as there were homicides (17,793).

Looking at this data, one can garner the realization that suicide, suicide ideations, and suicide attempts impact a great deal of the population nationwide and worldwide. This is not a matter that can easily be swept under a rug. Attention must be drawn to the fact that suicide affects all age groups, education levels, genders, gender affiliations, economic dispositions, and racial and cultural identities. I am cognizant that there are many causative factors associated with suicide, but in this work, I will primarily be focusing on depression and suicide. The possibility of suicide is most serious when a person has a plan for suicide that includes:
• Talking about wanting to die and kill oneself.
• Looking for a way to kill oneself.
• Talking about feeling hopeless or having no purpose.
• Talking about feeling trapped or being in unbearable pain.
• Talking about being a burden to others.
• Being depressed or having other mental issues.
• Increased social isolation.
• Significant changes in appearance and hygiene.
• Giving away valued possessions; making other preparations for death.
• A sudden change in mood.
• Increased alcohol and drug abuse.
• Previous suicide attempts.
• Access to means of suicide (possessing a gun or having a

quantity of pills).

Please understand that people who have suicidal thoughts may not seek help because they feel that they cannot be helped. I have often had those feelings and acted on those feelings in destructive manners. This is my story!

My story includes several suicide attempts that occurred when I found myself in major episodes. I am openly communicating this to help this book's readers, especially those seriously considering terminating their lives. My initial attempts were prior to my being cognizant of the fact I was living with clinical depression. I was in a severe crisis event that caused me to want to give up on life. The inner pain lasted for weeks, and all I could think of was putting an end to it all. I did not think of my significant other or my children but felt that my life was worthless and the stress too great to continue on with life.

I was still active and functioning well at the church but totally devoid of any feelings and just wanted to end it all. I started taking sleeping pills, which resulted in my, after many attempts, overdosing and being taken to a hospital. Regretfully, I was discharged with no referrals to anyone. I continued abusing pills until I'd had enough of feeling hopeless and took the necessary steps to get hospitalized at a major private mental facility 150 miles from my home. I was open and honest in my treatment and thought that I needed detoxing from the sleeping pills.

After a few days, a team of psychiatrists met with me and shared that I did not have a problem with sleeping pills and, after conversing with me, diagnosed me with clinical depression. They did a thorough job of explaining the disease to me. After examining my family history and my personal history, they were very confident that I had severe clinical depression. A few days later I was discharged with a sound treatment plan for ongoing care back home. They assisted me in getting a good psychiatrist and psychologist, and I invested myself in my treatment for many years. I adjusted well to my antidepressants and experienced very few side affects. For years, I managed my depression well, with very little tweaking to my medications, until October of 2015.

Having lived and battled with my depression for seventeen years, I was able to live a productive and fruitful life. Marital dysfunctions, life stressors, and the death of my parents during that period did not cause any serious depressive episodes. I assertively for years was aggressive in seeking out help from my therapeutic team. In, August of 2012, I relocated and retired to South Florida. I was doing well until the beginning of October 2015, at which time I went into a long, fifteen-month, painful and exhaustive period, which resulted in three suicide attempts and two hospitalizations. This could have been avoided if I had only reached out to my support team.

In retrospect, I allowed myself to enter this destructive period knowing that I was sinking into this deep, dark period of depression. I submitted to the situation and circumstances that were the causative factors into my descent into this long period of depression. In submitting, I found myself in a world of trouble. Once in this vicious cycle, I felt hopeless and believed that there was no way out. In that frame of mind, you make one poor decision after another. The symptoms of depression were apparent, but I continued my course of denial of those feelings. Fellow longtime sufferers of depression will tell you that that once depression starts knocking at your door, you are totally aware of what's up the road. You become stuck, ignore the feeling, and refuse to reach out, and then the battle starts all over again. I have told depression, "Come on," many times, intellectually and emotionally thinking I could overcome sinking into that dark, dismal, dysfunctional, and destructive pit of depression.

I take full responsibility for not extracting that negative force from my life and for not going to my psychiatrist and psychologist when I should have gone prior to the initial onset of the problem. It is almost as if I wanted to be in this season of depression. The result of not reaching out was a fourteen-month extensive battle with severe clinical depression that led to three suicide attempts and two hospitalizations. During this time frame, the struggles and self-inflictions were enormous. Mere words in print, however, are never a clear characterization of the actual impact that a major relapse into clinical depression can have on one's life, and the person's desire for cessation of life.

It is only by the grace of God, my support team, friends, and of course, my three loving and caring children, who demonstrated enduring and tough love at the time, that I am still here and no longer in a depressed state. I am penning these words in honor of those who helped me at this juncture in my life, and I take great personal satisfaction in knowing that there is an inner self that causes me to fight every day on this journey.

I empathize and sympathize with those of you who need help with the disease but do not have those forces of love surrounding you and a support team to turn to in your battle with depression. Remember, by assertively reaching out or sharing with a significant other that your life is out of control and that you are contemplating suicide or have attempted suicide, you do not have to succumb to these feelings. The fact that I am in the ministry did not deter me from attempting suicide. People from all walks of life, economic dispositions, professions, racial heritages, families, and all ages attempt or commit suicide because of depression. Those who tell you that you are going to hell if you commit suicide are fostering a lie according to my understanding of God. You have a debilitating disease that is out of your control without proper management, treatment, and medication. God is aware of that and loves you, anyway!

There are people in place to assist and guide you through those feelings of despondency, who will become assets to you in your struggle. It is because God wants you to make the best of your life that he has placed those angels there to be there in your battle with depression. I have delivered eulogies for those who have committed suicide, and I have never cast judgment on their eternal destiny. To assign people residency in hell because of suicide is a sad commentary on the current state of religion in our world.

Silence is the worst enemy to confront and deal with depression and suicidal ideations. Most people who attempt suicide do not die from their attempt, but the risk is much higher of completing suicide in relation to those who have never attempted suicide. Given the finality of suicide, the need for treatment is all the more important. When I'm in my depression, darkness, despair, self-imposed loneliness, and detachment overwhelm me. I have no recollection of the reality of days or weeks or months when I am in an extensive period of depression. This leads to increased thoughts of suicide, and eventually acting upon those thoughts.

While in depression, nothing goes right and I view myself as a complete failure despite the fact that I function well outside of my own reality. My mind and body suffer from constant exhaustion, and I find no pleasure in anything. This is the time when one must proactively seek outside inference and guidance. If you find yourself at this point, do not try to go it alone. Reach out for help. If you don't have a medical and psychological team in place, and family members to assist and confront you, then call or contact one of the following suicide prevention agencies.

- American Association of Suicidology - 202-247-2280
www.suicidology.org
- American Association for Suicide Prevention
www.afsp.org
- Jason Foundation
www.jasonfoundation.com
- National Suicide Prevention Hotline 800-SUICIDE (784-2433) www.suicide.org
- National Suicide Prevention Lifeline 800-273-TALK (8255)
- Society for the Prevention of Teen Suicide
www.sptsusa.com
- Suicide Prevention Advocacy Network (SPAN)
www.spanusa.org

There are suicide prevention hotlines and advocacy groups based on your age, gender, nationality, sexual orientation, and professional disciplines.

Many people cannot perceive of or understand why we would contemplate or attempt suicide. The people who feel that way are not living in our shoes and do not understand our desire to escape from the reality of life. For us, there seems to be no difference between life or death, especially when we are at the height of a depressive period. It's exhaustive and saps us of our energy and will to live. The feelings of emptiness associated with depression are extremely difficult to overcome. Living with an enormous amount of emotional pain becomes a daily nightmare. Yet, our hope resides in reaching out to others, acknowledging our hopeless feelings, and developing the coping skills that will enable us to fight through these tough times.

Please stay alive, fight this battle, and live your life to the fullest. Your survival resides in your desire to move from the ash heap of depression and clear and cleanse your mind from suicide ideations and suicide attempts. Trust me, it can be accomplished.

CHAPTER 7
THE AUTHOR'S CHILDREN SPEAK

Gilbert III:

Twenty years ago, our father was diagnosed with clinical depression. That day forever changed our lives. We were in utter disbelief. How could this happen? Our father, whom we lovingly refer to as "Daddy," is one of the strongest people we know, and he's the one always helping to counsel and uplift others. He courageously shared this with our entire family and even researched and realized that he was sure certain deceased family members had suffered in silence from depression. He was determined to not let this disease define him in a negative manner but to embrace it and use his experience to assist others.

When I was growing up as the firstborn child and only boy, my dad was, as he has always been, my hero and best friend, along with my mother. I vividly remember growing up in Philly as a young child and travelling all over the city with my dad. This included going to every major sporting event in Philadelphia and also shadowing him to work as a senior pastor. We would go from hospital to hospital as my dad was visiting with sick members of the church, praying for them, and providing uplifting and encouraging words. Daddy also had a second job as a counselor working with recovering drug addicts. My favorite childhood movie was Superman, and that's who my dad was to me. He was invincible and always came to the rescue of others.

During my early teenage years, Daddy accepted a job as senior pastor of a church in Norfolk, VA. I was crushed that we were leaving my beloved Philly and moving to Virginia. My dad promised me and my family that we would be okay and that he would make sure that we had a support system. He continued to do God's work and saved countless lives in this role. One experience that I will never forget was when my dad got a phone call in the middle of the night from a grieving family. They had just learned that their twelve-year-old son had drowned on a vacation with friends out of town. I asked him, "How do you have the strength to meet with this family, and what do you tell someone who has lost a child?"

He said, "Son, this is one of the hardest aspects of my job, but God has called me to assist others in the grieving process and help them put the pieces of their lives back together over time." He continued to do this amazing work until he suffered from a heart attack and was forced to retire as a senior pastor.

Fast forward—I'm now a thirty-seven-year-old man. My dad and I remain extremely close, and we talk on a daily basis. He now lives in South Florida, which was his retirement dream, to move somewhere warm and play golf every day. You would think that living the "dream" retirement life would cure his depression. However, that's not how this cruel disease works. Depression is like any other chronic lifelong disease such as asthma, migraines, diabetes, and so on.

I do not suffer from depression, and I've tried my best over the years to learn as much about the disease to better support my dad and others who have it. Watching someone you love suffer in silence, when there isn't really much that you can do to fix it right away, is painful. I'm naturally a fixer and try to rationalize with my dad to "snap out of it," but that's not how depression works. It's taken him sharing with us openly and honestly that while our hearts are in the right place, you can't just shake depression. We have learned to be supportive and have learned the importance of just being there when he is suffering a bout of depression. We also talk to our dad daily and keep a pulse on how he is feeling. Wanting an immediate solution, when there is none, to curing a bout of depression in a loved one is the hardest part for family members to accept. It's a journey and a process, but with the appropriate support system and love, your loved one will beat this disease. Just be patient and understanding.

Today, my dad is in a much better place because he understands the disease that he will forever live with. He still has his bouts of depression, but he has set up a support system of psychiatrists, psychologists, and his family and friends to support him during these rough periods. He is living out his greatest purpose from God, and that is to be a living testimony to help others dealing with depression to cope and survive. He has shared that his only goal from this book is to save one life. Watching this man help others throughout my life, I know that he will go on to save thousands of lives. We are so proud of Daddy for being a vocal leader for a disease that many are afraid to speak out about. It is our sincere hope and prayer that this book will help your loved one or you learn to be part of their support system.

Erica:

Daddy. My hero. My first love. Strong. Loving. Caring. Passionate. Intelligent. Stubborn. Tough. Provider. The aforementioned are just a small sampling of the words that come to mind when I think about my father. Growing up and living with a father with clinical depression has molded me into the person I am today.

Many people question why I chose to become a physician. My typical response always includes memories of my childhood days tagging along with my daddy to various hospitals, nursing homes, and parishioners' homes. Most children would find that boring, but I was always intrigued. The human body, mind, and spirit are amazing things. However, I always fail to discuss how my father's struggle with clinical depression helped mold me into the physician I am today.

To get to that point, let's go back to the beginning. My earliest childhood memories of my father are great. He was always present and worked hard to ensure that his three children were provided with the best opportunities and start in life. Even more than the tangible things we received, I most treasure the time he spent with us, and planting the seeds for our faith in God. Yes, my father is a pastor, but he never forced religion on us. Yes, we went to church, and he knew of the great powers of Christ, but he allowed all of us to forge that very personal relationship for ourselves. And for that, I'm forever grateful. God is my Savior and refuge. I would not be here without the love of Christ. But I was blessed to develop that relationship when my soul was ready. Thank you, Daddy.

Getting back to depression: I always saw my dad as this larger-than-life pastor who I was, and still am, in awe of. Despite his many ups and downs, I wholeheartedly believe that he was born to spread God's message. A message of hope. A message of God's greatness. Most importantly, a message that strong Black men can suffer from depression and still lead a productive life. In our society, men (especially African-American men) are expected to be fearless and not show emotion. However, numerous research studies and lost lives have shown quite the opposite. We are all human. We all feel. Depression hurts.

My tough and larger-than-life father is one such example. The first time I remember my father being depressed was around the time when I was eleven or twelve, but I still remember the next part of the story like it was yesterday: my father's first suicide attempt. What happened next is a blur.

I remember chaos.

I remember crying.

I remember screaming.

I remember thinking my daddy was going to die.

I remember trying to keep my little sister calm.

I remember my mother's pleas and tears.

Despite all that, my father got in the car and drove off. To where? I will never know.

A few painful hours later, he came back. He came back in tears. My parents made up, and my dad ended up sick in the restroom, but to the glory of God, he was alive! I do remember him going "away" to Washington DC after this event to get better. I didn't know it was a psychiatric hospital. I just knew he went away to "de-stress." He came back a different man. He was happier. Things seem to go back to normal until the next fight. Little did I know that this would be first of many such periodic episodes over the years. However, I must say that despite all of this, my father never made us (his children) feel less loved or valued. Thank you, Daddy! I know that was hard.

My last year, in college, I too received the same news: I had been diagnosed with anxiety and depression. My diagnosis and treatment were rather swift since my family already knew the signs and symptoms from my father. Though I have my ups and downs, therapy and medication allow me to live a great life. I know what to expect and how to navigate the lows and highs.

Now let's fast forward to my most recent and, God willing, last memory of my father attempting to end his life. It was last year, 2016. I was transitioning from residency to fellowship. Around 6 or 7 pm CST, I received a phone call from my father. Not just any call. A distressed call while he was in his psychiatrist's office. He was angry that his psychiatrist would not allow him to go home. After chatting with his doctor, I found out that my dad had attempted suicide via sleeping pills a day or so prior. I'd had no idea.

I felt so helpless and guilty that I was not there, and that I had not realized that he was in such a dark place. After coordinating with his doctor (in South Florida), an inpatient psychiatrist in Washington, DC (where my siblings live, and where he would have more support, as I was living in Houston), and my older brother, we were able to safely arrange for him to transport to DC for a much-needed hospitalization. After this hospitalization and walking away from a toxic relationship, my father has been a changed man.

Now, I'm not naïve. I know that depression is a lifelong battle, but how you approach it has everything to do with how the rest of your life will be. You have two choices: give up or keep fighting. My father finally chose the latter. He finally realized that it takes a village, and being honest helps ease some of the burden. I have tears of joy as I write this because I see a different side of my father today: a man at peace, a man who is brave enough to share a very personal story with the world in hopes of saving one life. His story has inspired me to be open with my struggle.

Depression is real, and common.

Never be ashamed to seek help. Mental health is just as important as, if not more so than, physical health. You can't take care of your body if your mind is sick. Life is worth living if you find your "village" and take it one day at a time. God bless!

Lauren:

I've always had a unique relationship with my dad. When I was growing up, my dad was my own personal superhero. I nicknamed him "Daddyman with the master plan." The nickname was very fitting. I didn't see my dad as the busy pastor who was working on his Doctor of Ministry degree, volunteering, visiting the sick, and secretly battling depression. I was too young to see it or understand it. I knew my dad had bad moods at times, but I didn't care. I was the the baby of the family, who was sassy, outspoken, and mischievous. I just figured I was pushing the envelope, which was not uncommon for me.

My dad was the fun dad. He was the dad who sang, "If you're happy and you know it, clap your hands," in the mornings as he was dropping me off at school. I used to sneak up the stairs to the room over the garage (our playroom/his office) while he was in there reading or working on a sermon. I would break into a rhythmless dance, which always made my dad laugh. He would say, "Shake it, Mama," and in return I would giggle and dance even harder. I would wait to hear the garage door open because that meant Daddy was home, and he usually had candy.

He would take my friends and me to the water park every year to celebrate the last day of school. Every summer we would go on a four-week family vacation to a cool new destination. That was always a summer highlight. Every Sunday after church I would follow my dad around. I stood behind him as he would hug and say goodbye to members of the church. As a result, I was nicknamed "the shadow."

Christmas season was my favorite time of the year. We would play Christmas music as we all decorated the house. We would wake up to Nat King Cole and an entire room of gifts. I didn't see depression. I saw Daddyman. I had an awesome childhood. I had two parents who were very hands-on and loving. I commend my dad for pushing through whatever he was struggling with to be a damn good dad.

One memory sticks out in my mind. I remember my dad lying on the steps leading up to the room over the garage. It was the first time in my life I saw him crying. He had attempted suicide. I didn't understand what was happening around me. I just knew something wasn't right. My mom and siblings were freaking out. The rest is a blur. I don't remember what happened that evening. I vaguely remember my dad leaving to go "out of town" afterward. I do remember family watching us while my mom and dad were out of town. I had a ball. I got to eat more junk food, stay up later, and get away with things that my parents would have caught on to. I realize now that my dad was away seeking treatment. I don't recall anyone explaining anything to me. I didn't care. I was a kid who was oblivious.

I feel guilty that I missed all the signs that something was wrong with my dad. As an adult, I realize there were signs. My dad was going inward while being alone in the room over the garage, my parents weren't getting along, my dad would go inward at times during vacation, and at Christmas I vaguely remember him having "moods." He was a man struggling with depression.

It became glaring to me as an adult. My siblings and I began to have conversations to check to see if Daddy was okay. That was a normal part of life. We just wanted to make sure that he wasn't in a funk, and we would discuss ways to get him out of his funk. The worst year was 2016. That year I found out that my dad again had attempted to take his life. I cried for what seemed like an eternity. I cried because I had missed the signs of him wanting to end his life; I cried because I never thought he would do that; I cried because I hurt for him; I cried because I couldn't picture life without him; I cried because I wished we could take on whatever was causing him so much pain. This was followed by two more attempts.

These were the hardest moments of my life. I didn't understand how a man surrounded by so much love and who has achieved so much would want to end his life. Why would he want to leave us?

I was angry that he didn't tell us it was getting that bad. I was devastated that he was suffering. I don't want my dad to suffer. I love him so much. I can't picture life without my superhero. I feel guilt. I can't think of a time that my dad wasn't here for us. We weren't there for him to catch this. This is my biggest worry. I don't know what I would do if I received a call that I'd lost my dad. I dread it, and I pray that it doesn't happen.

I worry so much. I want to fix the man who fixed everyone else. I hope writing will be a release for him. He wants to write to tell his story and to remove the idea that mental health issues are something for the weak. Selfishly, I just want this to be the release that allows him to talk openly and provide the relief that he has needed. I commend him for his honesty and his bravery. He is speaking out about an issue that no one wants to address, but everyone has been affected by, either the person himself or herself directly, or someone in his or her life.

CHAPTER 8
THIS IS MY SONG

I truly believe that everybody's life is a song. My life has been a song with several refrains ranging from sad to happy. Living with clinical depression has been an extreme challenge for me throughout the years fraught with many lows and highs. Looking back over the years, I have experienced many fruitful and productive days. I am proud of the many professional, academic, and life goals that I have achieved in spite of my depression.

Depression has not kept me from being the person I am, and through God's grace I have touched and changed many lives. My ministry has always been one challenging others, changing lives, and fostering healing in the many people I have been fortunate to pastor and love. I would like to spend the rest of my life's journey singing to those who are struggling with depression, singing the song that tells you that you can live with this disease, and you can also have a song to sing.

The ability to sing your song resides within you. You have to accept the reality of the disease in your life and take the necessary steps forward and remain dutiful and faithful to the good treatment plan mapped out for you by your support team. Please keep in mind that you will never to be able to conquer or defeat depression, and that coping with the disease is an ongoing treatable battle. The mere fact that you have acknowledged that you are living with depression and need the assistance of others and your medications daily to sustain you is a good thing. Remember, relapse often occurs when we become overly confident that we are in complete control of the disease. Relapse raises its ugly head when we feel as though we are on top of the world. It happens because we forget to continue to the do the things that allowed us to make it through a difficult period.

Depression is a disease that requires us to manage our lifestyle, avoid people who have a tendency to bring us down, and find positive things to do daily. I have found that I can go years without a major depressive bout as long as I keep in perspective that I still am living with clinical depression. I never forget my medicines and am always aware of the importance of assessing my mental and physical health. This is an ongoing process that must be followed and has helped me to maintain my well-being. I have family and close friends who are aware of my depression and who confront me when they realize that I may be going inward. I respect and welcome their challenges to me, and this affords me the insurance and assurance of knowing that I am not alone in this struggle. Those who reach out to us are caring and loving in how they reach out. This is not a daily occurrence but a systemic approach to assist me on my journey.

I want to encourage you to remember that it is normal in life, living with depression or not, that we all have dysfunctions and problems. These issues must be faced head-on and are not always a result of our depression. Avoiding the daily and periodic stresses of life is not healthy and may lead us into a relapse. I confront those issues head-on and reach out to my support team for guidance. Living with depression requires that we see a therapist regularly to converse on matters pertaining to us, and this will not allow us to internalize our struggles. It is my impression that when we take the "Lone Ranger" approach, the greater our anxiety becomes, which leads to the onset of a depressive period. Our ability to sing our song resides in our desire to be open and expressive of the "stuff" we internalize. All human beings must take the "pressure cooker" approach to life. Steam must be released from the pressure cooker, or the top will explode, and without positive avenues to release what we internalize, the result is negative explosions of our emotions and feelings. Failing to release affects our self-worth, energy level, motivation, and our mood. To express and vent what we are feeling means that we are singing in and through our storms. Life is so much easier when we release the internal, even in small matters.

The stigma of depression should not make us feel as though we are damaged. As the stigma continues, we must go on discussing our disease openly, leaving the judgment behind. I have found that happiness is fleeting, temporary, and often outside of ourselves. Tragedy happens to all of us, trauma happens to all of us, and we have to accept this as a reality of life. We must focus on cultivating a meaningful life filled with rewarding relationships, food, and finding joy in the smaller matters of life.

I don't want people to treat me differently because I have depression. I faithfully take my medications every day of my life. It's very similar to taking medications for heart disease, hypertension, or any other physical malady. Without my medication, I have no interest in day-to-day living. Without medication, it is hard to maintain relationships with close family and friends. Without medication, I have feelings of overwhelming sadness. I find no happiness in the things that otherwise bring me joy. Society does not blame anyone for having physical illnesses. I wish there were more understanding surrounding depression and other mental illnesses. My hope is to create a little more understanding around this issue.

Please remember, depression is not our fault. With proper supportive treatment, it is only a temporary condition. You will get better and feel better about yourself. It is important that you take back control over your life and be responsible for your well-being. In taking control of my life, I have learned that there are things I can do and other things I cannot do. Taking responsibility for my life gives me the power to work out and work through whatever confronts me on the journey. Depression has caused me to reflect back over my life, focus on the now, and look positively toward the future with a determination that there is a power within me that will enhance my personal growth. I know now that everything around me is the direct effect of who I am at the moment.

We all desire peace and contentment; but it starts with finding within us the strength to forgive ourselves. Family and friends will forgive us the pain and hurt we have caused them, if we are honest and sincere in dealing with the disease. The difficulty resides in our inability to forgive ourselves in a manner that is therapeutic and helpful. The hardest thing to do on our path to living healthy lives is to be honest and realize that our putting forth the effort to feel and get better resides in us. Depression when diagnosed is not a life sentence to a prison of inner hell. We can free ourselves by forgiving the issues of our past and the pain of living with the disease.

This is my story! In telling my story, I have risked a great deal. I have welcomed others into my life by sharing my battle with depression. In telling my story, I have tried to be honest and forthcoming in order to save one life and assist others who are living with depression. The underlying causative factors of your depression are external: death, family dysfunctions, loss of job, aging, divorce, seasonal or internal factors, and chemical abnormalities. The diagnosis is not terminal, and suicide is not the answer. One can live a rewarding and fruitful life, even with depression. Sing your song and live your life.

This is my song, and I am singing it by telling my story!